Contents

Some words are shown in bold, **like this**. They are explained in "Words to Know" on page 23.

What is a community?

A **community** is a group of people with something in common. A community could be a group of people who live in the same area or who can speak the same language.

People in the Community

People Who Help Us

Rebecca Rissman

www.raintreepublishers.co.uk
Visit our website to find out more information about Raintree books.

To order:

☎ Phone 0845 6044371
📄 Fax +44 (0) 1865 312263
📠 Email myorders@raintreepublishers.co.uk

Customers from outside the UK please telephone +44 1865 312262

Raintree is an imprint of Capstone Global Library Limited, a company incorporated in England and Wales having its registered office at 7 Pilgrim Street, London, EC4V 6LB – Registered company number: 6695582

Edited by Rebecca Rissman, Siân Smith, Charlotte Guillain, and Vaarunika Dharmapala
Designed by Kimberly Miracle
Picture research by Tracy Cummins and Kim Tidwell
Originated by Steve Walker, Capstone Global Library Ltd
Printed and bound in China by Leo Paper Products Ltd

ISBN 978 0 431194 34 9 (hardback)
14 13 12 11 10
10 9 8 7 6 5 4 3 2 1

ISBN 978 1 406 24681 0 (paperback)
15 14 13 12 11
10 9 8 7 6 5 4 3 2

British Library Cataloguing in Publication Data
Rissman, Rebecca.
People who help us. -- (Acorn plus)
1. Human services--Juvenile literature. 2. Service industries--Juvenile literature.
A full catalogue record for this book is available from the British Library

Acknowledgements
We would like to thank the following for permission to reproduce photographs: Age Fotostock **p. 15 left** (© Jeremy Woodhouse); Alamy **pp. 5 right** (© GoGo Images Corporation), **14 right** (© Nancy G Fire Photography, Nancy Greifenhagen), **18** (© Ariel Skelley), **19 middle** (© Juniors Bildarchiv), **19 right** (© Olaf Doering); Corbis **p. 21** (© Lucy Nicholson/Reuters); Getty Images **pp. 8 left** (The Image Bank/Yellow Dog Productions Inc.), **8 right** (Stone/Bruce Foster), **9 right** (Royalty Free), **10** (Somos/Veer), **11 left** (Mike Powell), **13** (Karin Dreyer), **16 left** (Tom Stoddart Archive/Hulston Archive), **17 right** (Alexander Hassenstein/Staff), **22 left** (Karin Dreyer); istockphoto **pp. 6** (© aldomurillo), **12** (© Nathan Gleave); Photolibrary **pp. 4** (Photodisc/© Glen Allison), **11 right** (© Thomas Barwick); Shutterstock **pp. 5 left** (© Mikhail Levit), **7** (© Philip Lange), **9 left** (© salamanderman), **14 left** (© Steve Noakes), **15 right** (© Fiorentini Massimo), **19 left** (© Mark William Penny), **20** (© Ron Hilton), **22 middle** (© Mark William Penny), **31 right** (© Steve Noakes).

Cover photograph of a school teacher sitting with pupils in Sri Lanka reproduced with permission of Getty Images/© Hugh Sitton . Back cover photograph of firemen with a burning car reproduced with permission of Shutterstock/© Ron Hilton.

We would like to thank Nancy Harris and Adriana Scalise for their invaluable help in the preparation of this book.

Every effort has been made to contact copyright holders of material reproduced in this book. Any omissions will be rectified in subsequent printings if notice is given to the publishers.

A community could be a group of people who have the same religion or who go to the same school. People can be part of lots of different communities at the same time.

Some **communities** are very big. A whole country can be a community. Some communities are small.
A family or a group of friends can be a community.

When people talk about the community, they usually mean a group of people who live in the same area.

Working in the community

People in the **community** help each other when they work at different jobs. People work to **earn** money. The jobs they do help people in different ways.

goods

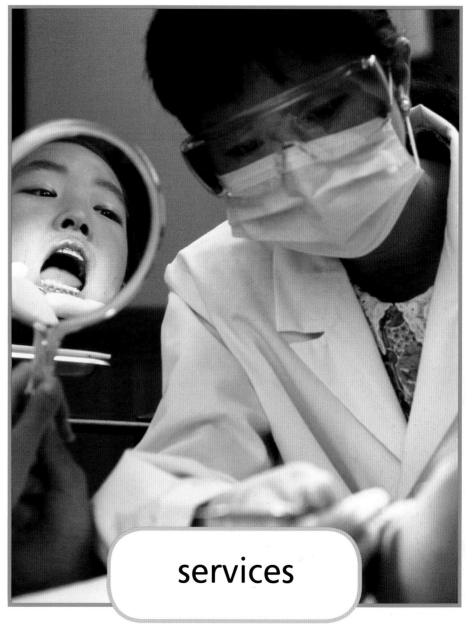

services

Some people work by selling **goods**. Goods are things people need to eat or use. Some people work by selling **services**. Services are jobs done for other people.

People who help us stay healthy

Doctors help people in the **community** stay healthy. Doctors help when people are sick. Doctors help when people are hurt.

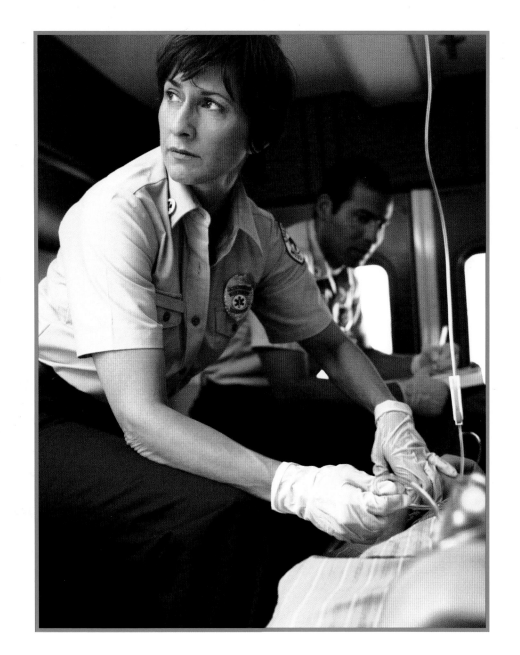

Paramedics work with doctors. Paramedics help **patients** get to the doctor. Nurses work with doctors. Nurses help care for patients.

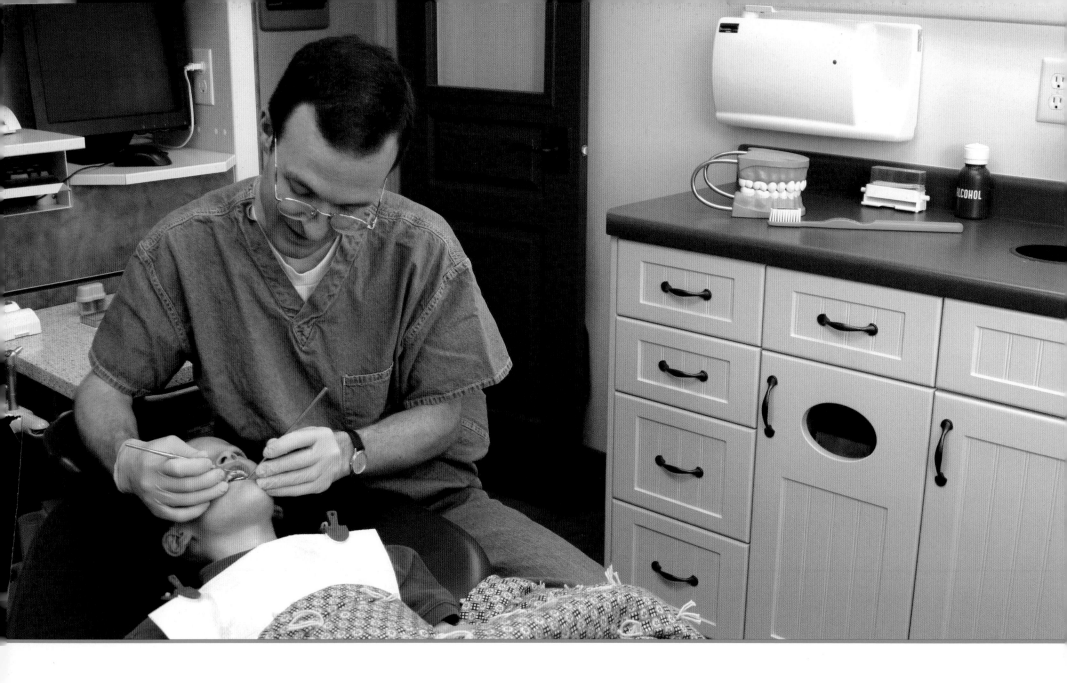

Dentists also help people in the **community** stay healthy. Dentists check people's teeth. Dentists help care for people's teeth.

Hygienists work with dentists. Hygienists help to clean people's teeth. Hygienists show people how to clean their teeth.

People who help us stay safe

Firefighters help people in the **community** stay safe.
Firefighters put out fires. Firefighters help people to
escape from fires.

Police officers help people in the community stay safe. Police officers keep drivers safe. Police officers **arrest** people who break the law. They help fight **crime**.

People who help others learn

Teachers help people in the **community** to learn.
Teachers teach students many different **subjects**.
Teachers teach **facts** and different **skills**.

Coaches help people in the community to learn.
Coaches teach people how to play different sports.
Coaches help people to stay healthy, too.

People who help animals

Vets help animals to stay healthy. Vets help animals that are sick.

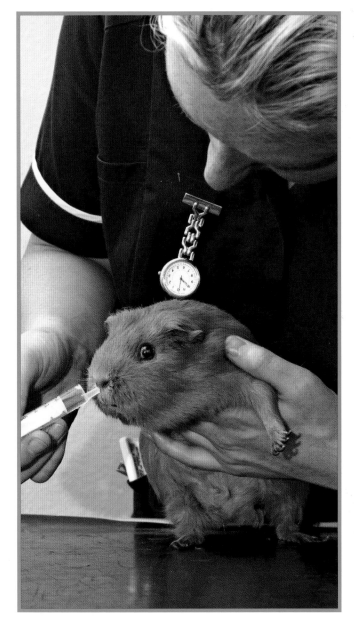  

Vets help pets, farm animals, and zoo animals. Vets help the **community** by caring for our animals.

Working together

All the different jobs people do in the **community** are important. We can do a lot more when we work together than when we work by ourselves.

Helping each other and working together makes life better for everyone.

Community helpers

How do the people in these pictures help their **community**?

1

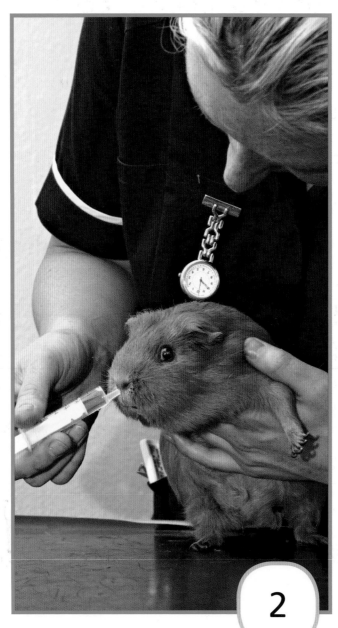

2

3

Answers on page 24.

Words to know

arrest   to be held by the police

community   group of people with something in common. A community can be a group of people who live in the same area.

crime   something against the rules. People commit crimes when they break a law.

earn   to get something for work. People earn money for work.

fact   piece of information

goods   things that people eat or use. Food, toys, and clothing are goods.

paramedic   someone who helps transport people to see the doctor

patient   someone who is cared for at the hospital or dentist's office

services   jobs people do for each other. Serving food, cleaning a house, and driving a bus are services.

skill   the ability to do something. Riding a bike is a skill.

subject   something people study in school. Science is a subject.

Index

Note to parents and teachers

Before reading:

Tell children that a community is a group of people. There are many different and similar communities around the world. Some communities are schools, families, neighbourhoods, religious groups, and work places. Ask children to brainstorm a list of people who help the community. Create a chart of their ideas. As children are sharing their ideas, ask them why we need each person in our community.

After reading:

• Divide children into different types of community workers: a person who helps us stay healthy, stay safe, helps others learn, and who helps animals. Ask them to make a list with their group about things their community worker does. Then they can make a skit and/or poster that describes their community worker. Children can make props, costumes, and pictures to aid their performance.

• Talk to the children about the job they would like to have when they are older. Children can write or draw a picture about the job they are interested in.

Answers to questions on page 22

Photo 1 shows a hygienist helping people to keep their teeth clean.
Photo 2 shows a vet caring for an animal.
Photo 3 shows firefighters putting out a fire.